GW00986501

meow the cat

universe publishing

contents

That's a **looong** way up—
lucky I have **nine lives**!

Don't let these **claws** fool you.
Inside, I'm a real **pussycat**.

Now??

C'mon, I just got comfortable.

Awwrighty. High-four!

Shh.

I'm trying to catch

a few hours

of **shut-eye**

before bedtime.

Man! I almost forgot how good **goldfish** tasted.

You'll have to **excuse me**;
sometimes I get a little **frisky**.

Come here, little goldfish . . .

I just want to say "hi."

You think this is **crazy**—

I once fell asleep on the **dog**!

Quick question:

What does d o o f t a c spell?

My **therapist** says
I need to **let it all out**.

Ahhh, the purr-fect

catnap . . .

Sleeping?

No, I was just **resting** my eyes.

May I have this dance?

I know, I know.
I'm the **cutest** thing
you've **ever seen**.
Tell me something I don't know.

Ommmmm . . .

Meditating allows me
to become **one**
with my **inner kitten**.

I gotta start laying off that catnip. I'm seeing some weird things lately!

Here, let me **help you** with that can of **tuna**.

Let's see if I **can get** any more **uncomfortable** before hitting the sack.

I come in **peace**.

Take me to your **cat food**.

Forget **caterwauling**.

This is **caterwailing**.

Talk about
"Pet of the Month" material!

Put 'em up, put 'em up. Let's settle this like **cats**!

Nothing like a **good**

stretch after the fourth **nap** of the day.

Now **wait** a minute!

You can't **prove**

I knocked over that **fishbowl**.

Oh, yeah. Oh, yeah. Right there. That's the **spot**.

Don't **mind** me, little birdie,
just go about **your business**
and **forget** you ever **saw** me.

You got something **better** for me to do **than sleep**?

But enough about me—
have you noticed my
new colored lenses?

It's **tough** to
get by on just **eighteen hours**
of **sleep** a day.

Take **one** more step, pal, and
you'll be **wearing** this mitt.

Excuse me, but are you going to **finish** that tuna **sandwich**?

When I **open** my eyes,
that **dog** better
be **outta here**.

Beautiful, yes.

But I have a brain, too.

Don't forget to **wake me**
up for **lunch**, OK?

What?? I thought you said "mug" for the camera.

I **wonder** what
insomnia feels like.

Haven't you ever **heard**

of **cat yoga**?

Hmmm . . . Looks like lunch

is **hiding** behind the couch.

Wait! I've reconsidered;
I'll take the **leftovers** after all.

Please **hurry** back. I'll **miss** you.

cats in

thought

Who **you lookin' at**, pal?

Looks like if I **jump** from the **bookcase** to the **lamp,** I'll be **home free**.

I'm **ready** for my **close-up**, Mr. DeMille.

It was a **dark** and **stormy** night when **suddenly**…

I beg your **pardon**.
I answer only to **"Princess."**

You blinked first. I win!

Don't **worry** about me.
I'll probably just **take a nap**.

Get outta here!

She did *what?*

I'm as **gentle** as a lamb.

And I **look** like one, too.

Decisions, decisions.

Let's go with the string today.

Whadda you **mean,**

we're out of **catnip**?

Aha! So it's **you** who's been **clipping** my claws at night . . .

That **stuff** might work
with the **dogs**,
but you're **dealing** with a
highly **intelligent** cat here.

Hey, Daddy-o. I tell ya' that cat sure can jive and swing. You dig?

Did **anyone** just see

a **mouse** go by?

Hey! Who **moved** the yarn up to the **top shelf**?

Would it be **asking** too much
to **pick** me up some
real food instead of
that **canned stuff**?

We'd like you to **come down** to the station to **answer** a few **questions**, ma'am.

Must **find** catnip,

must find **catnip** . . .

Dahhling.
It's true **blondes** have more **fun**.

A dog?
What do we **need** a dog for?
I thought **everything**
was **great** between us.

Let me get this straight: first the milk, now the fish. What else are we out of?

Where do you **think** you're going with that **cage**?

That **better** be
the dog's **leash**!

I **heard** you're starting **trouble** with my brother. You lookin' for a **catfight**?

Fork over the **tuna** and

he can have his **ducky** back.

Here's **looking at you**, kit.

You won't be **gone long**, will you?

So I sez to the guy, I sez:

I don't want no trouble,

I just want what's mine, ya hear?

You try **playing** with a string for **twenty** minutes and not get **exhausted**.

No way! You said it wouldn't **hurt** last time, either.

There's a **tiger** inside me

just dying to **get out**.

Make **sure** you get my **right side**; it is my **best side** after all.

You want the **crazy face?**
I'll **give you** the crazy face!!

Whoa! You never said **anything** about bringing home a **puppy**!

Wow, look at that:

a reupholstered **couch**,

ripe for the **scratching** . . .

Me? I'm simply **content** to sit here and look **cute**.

I'm not **leaving** until I get

what I **came** for.

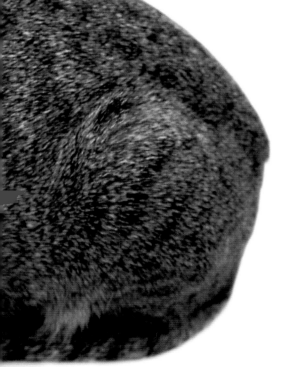

Let it be **known** that an Oriental Shorthair has never **lost** a staring contest— and I don't **plan** on being the **first**.

I'm going to **ask you one** more time: Where is the **ball of yarn**?

I don't **mean** to be **presumptuous**, but is that piece of **fish** spoken for?

Look at that **good-looking** cat staring back at **me**.

Did I ever **tell** you about the time I **fought** back three strays and a rabid **dog** for a half-eaten piece of **bologna**?

abyssinian

True to its sphinxlike appearance, the Abyssinians's heritage remains clouded in mystery. Some believe British soldiers brought it home following the Abyssinian War (ca. 1868), while others have traced its roots to India. Regardless, the incredibly intelligent and regal Aby—with its elegant body and almond-shaped eyes—is clearly identifiable today as one of the most desirable and loyal breeds.

american curl

A relative newcomer to the cat world, this breed first catches your attention by its curled-back ears (hence its name) that look more like cowlicks. As playful and friendly as any cat, the Curl is incredibly easygoing, thereby making it extremely popular in houses filled with children or other pets. With its unique ears and a tail as long as its rectangular body, many may feel that the Curl is slightly misshapen. But those fortunate enough to know this delightful creature will tell you that you'd be hard-pressed to find a more lovable cat to curl up with.

american shorthair

Believed to be a true blue blood due to its arrival on these shores via the Mayflower, this all-American cat lives a long, healthy, and happy life. Since coming to America, it has earned its reputation as a stellar "rat and mouser," whether on ships traversing the Atlantic or in its unofficial post at post offices across the country. A perennial favorite among cat lovers, this shorthair adores children and has a sweet disposition. That is, unless it's in the midst of a hunt.

Sleek and well muscled, this breed seems to glitter as it lopes across the room. The Bengal is the first documented cross between a domestic and a non-domestic (Asian leopard) cat. The object was to create a feline that looked like a leopard but had the disposition

bengal

of a house cat. Due to its jungle roots, the breed still possesses a little of its descendants' wild side. And since its ancestors survived by avoiding humans, this cat has a genetic shyness—except around water, where it never passes up an opportunity to make a splash.

189

burmese

If there ever was an animal that relied on the magic of its eyes to enchant, cajole, or beguile, it is the Burmese. These lively and playful cats feed on the warmth and affection of their owners. Yet their soft, soulful eyes belie their inevitable (and, ultimately, successful) goal of taking over a household and reigning supreme.

Call it "Persian Lite." Exotic Shorthairs
look like Persians, act like Persians, and if
they could, they'd probably talk like their
classy cousins. However, the Exotic
Shorthair was bred mainly to relieve its
owners of the laborious process of the
daily grooming required by picky Persians.
An endearing and peaceful breed that
seems unperturbed by life's travails,
the quiet and considerate Exotic is content
to give you your space—but still demands
constant attention and affection.

exotic shorthair

A cross between two esteemed breeds, the Himalayan has evolved into a blue-eyed beauty boasting a Persian personality and Siamese color. A loving creature that can't seem to get enough of its owners, the Himmy carries itself in an aristocratic fashion. This longhaired cat comes in a variety of colors that is

himalayan

restricted to the facial mask and the ears, tail, feet, and legs, with the body in various shades of white to fawn.

maine coon

True, it is exceptionally playful and affectionate, but this is one cat you don't want constantly jumping into your lap as most weigh more than twice the average feline. As America's first longhaired cat, this "Gentle Giant" is nothing more than an oversized, playful kitten. The Maine Coon is America's second most popular breed, and has evolved from a working-class feline to a catwalk-loving show cat. Given its yeomanly ethic, shaggy coat, and free-roaming nature, there's no doubt that this hardy breed hails from the rough terrain of Maine.

It is far and away the most popular of all cats: the mixed breed. Today, more than nine out of ten cats in the world are considered domestic shorthair, or mixed. As one would expect, this natural selection creates cats of all sizes, shapes, personalities, and color. And because they don't follow a purebred bloodline, the temperament of the mixed cat varies widely depending on its environment.

mix

munchkin

As the name indicates, these cats are as small as they get. America's first dwarf cat, the Munchkin has legs so short it's a wonder how it's able to stand or get around. Though their bushy coats require a great deal of grooming, these are generally very low-maintenance pets that continue to retain their kittenish ways long into adulthood. Especially endearing is the way the Munchkin will sit up—kangaroo-like—to play, listen, or simply peruse its surroundings.

norwegian forest cat

The kissing cousin of the Maine Coon, this hearty breed has carried on for centuries in Norwegian folklore and around the globe. First mate aboard many Viking ships, their large physique and thick coat made the Norwegians well suited for the Nordic seafaring and pillaging life. Today, the Norwegian remains an ideal traveling companion, and moves freely between climates: shedding coats when the weather gets hot, and even changing color from light to dark with the passing seasons.

ocicat

What was supposed to be an Aby-point Siamese, serendipitously turned out to be a golden-spotted, ivory kitten. Thus was born the first Ocicat. Named for its resemblance to the ocelot, a magnificent wild cat from Central and South Americas, the Ocicat may look the part, but it is hardly feral. They do require large spaces, or places to climb, but they are basically needy homebodies who will fetch, respond to voice commands, and even walk on a leash.

oriental

shorthair

With a loud voice, large ears, and an oversized personality, the only thing the Oriental Shorthair is short on is patience—if it's ever left alone. Playful and affectionate, the Oriental is a demonstrative pet that draws comparison to dogs for its obedient and willing nature. Like its Siamese relative, it moves with a quiet, athletic elegance. The chatty Oriental is also desperate to please, and expects the same from its owners. Highly inquisitive, this breed is not shy about letting its feelings known—good or bad.

persian

You'd think that its short body, stocky legs, and thick bones would make it a real "dog," but this comely creature is one beautiful cat. Long a favorite of British and Middle Eastern royalty, the Persian is now the king of cats in the United States. With its glorious, long-flowing coat, this aristo-cat can usually be found atop the winner's stand at cat shows nationwide. The Persian prefers a serene environment, and requires ongoing attention to keep its coat looking beautiful. It's a lifetime commitment many people gladly make.

ragdoll

Named for its proclivity to go completely limp when held, the Ragdoll is a fascinating character study. This powerfully built cat has an unbelievable tolerance for pain, exhibits little or no fear, and remains incredibly loving and loyal—as long as it's repaid in kind. They like to play rough, but at the same time, they are very considerate and well behaved. They'll follow their humans everywhere with a soft musical voice, waiting patiently to once again melt in their owners' arms.

Despite the powerful, intriguing names that this breed has gone by over the

russian blue

years—Archangel, Maltese, and Russian—this gentle little cat with vivid green eyes is surprisingly demure and reserved. Bordering on the brink of extinction during World War II, the breed was revived with some Siamese mixing. Preferring cleanliness and order over disarray, this angel with the plush blue coat evinces a loving and quiet disposition.

scottish fold

It has been said that this breed perfectly combines a British sense of propriety with an American sense of hubris. The Scottish Fold has a massive round head that features a wide distance between the ears. And what ears! Folded forward, the ears give this breed a certain mischievous look. The ideal cat for apartment living, this sweet-tempered and affectionate feline is always eager to please.

For centuries they served admirably as "watch cats" in Russian monasteries as their agility, speed, and girth made them well suited to canvas the shadowy interiors after dark. Their appearance is what one would expect from a breed that calls Siberia home: a thick topcoat to repel rain and snow, and a dense undercoat to block gale-force winds. Renowned for their doglike loyalty and disposition, the

siberian forest cat

Siberian has remarkable jumping ability for a cat that resembles a linebacker more than a ballerina.

Smaller than most cats, this breed hails from the streets of Singapore, and is probably the result of the wild mating of Abyssinians and Burmese-type cats. Today, this quiet, yet very active feline has risen in stature to become the national cat of Malaysia. Distinguished by its giant eyes that seem out of proportion to its small frame, the Singapura becomes deeply attached to its owner, who is inevitably kept busy by this playfully curious cat.

singapura

Despite its African name, this breed hails from the exotic land of Canada. Considered by many to be the closest modern descendant of the

somali

sacred cats of ancient Egypt, the Somali resembles its shorthaired relative, the Abyssinian. Its wild, feral look adds to this cat's fascinating allure. Overly playful and inquisitive, Somalis seem to have an endless supply of energy and a ceaseless need for human companionship.

the cats